Government Queensland

Catalogue of the natural and industrial products of Queensland,

1873

Government Queensland

Catalogue of the natural and industrial products of Queensland, 1873

ISBN/EAN: 9783743339057

Manufactured in Europe, USA, Canada, Australia, Japa

Cover: Foto ©ninafisch / pixelio.de

Manufactured and distributed by brebook publishing software
(www.brebook.com)

Government Queensland

Catalogue of the natural and industrial products of Queensland,

1873

INTERNATIONAL EXHIBITION OF VIENNA, 1873.

CATALOGUE

OF THE

Natural and Industrial Products

OF

QUEENSLAND.

Governor :

THE MARQUIS OF NORMANBY.

Colonial Secretary :

ARTHUR HUNTER PALMER, Esquire.

Commissioners :

WALTER HILL. | KARL THEODOR STAIGER.
P. R. GORDON.

Agent-General :

R. DAINTREE.

BRISBANE:

BY AUTHORITY: JAMES C. BEAL, GOVERNMENT PRINTER.

1873.

INTRODUCTION.

THE Colony of Queensland forms the north-eastern corner of the great Australian continent, and embraces an area of 678,000 square miles. Its southern boundary commences at Point Danger, in latitude 28° 8' S., and traverses the mountain range which divides the waters of the Logan and Brisbane Rivers from those of the Tweed, Richmond, and Clarence, in a westerly direction, to the Great Dividing Range; when it takes a southerly course to the heads of the Barwon River, and then down that stream until the 29th parallel of latitude is reached, in longitude 149° 10'. Thence following that parallel westerly to the 141st meridian of longitude—the eastern boundary of South Australia—thence by that meridian to the 26th parallel; thence west by that parallel to long. 138°, and by that meridian north to the Gulf of Carpentaria; and by the sea-coast on the north and east.

The population of Queensland, at 31st December, 1871, was 125,146. The population, according to the Census taken in April, 1861 (sixteen months after the date of separation from New South Wales), was 30,059, so that the increase for ten years has been over 95,000.

Queensland is very rich in metals and minerals. The gold exported seaward from the colony during the year 1871 was 171,942 ozs., of the value of £619,160.

The gold fields are situated at intervals along the range dividing the waters flowing to the east coast from those trending westerly ; from the southern boundary of the colony to latitude 15° S., or over 14 degrees latitude.

Copper, lead, zinc, and antimony are found over the same space. A large number of Copper Mines have recently been opened up, but as the working has principally been confined to preliminary operations, copper does not figure as a large item in our exports, the quantity exported in 1871 having only been 3,029½ tons.

Tin is abundant in the district of Stanthorpe, which occupies an area of about 30 miles square, the centre of which is in lat. 28° 45'; long. 149° 50'. Tin has also been found at the head of the Burdekin, lat. 18° 30'; long. 151° 10'.

Mercury has been found in large deposits at the head of the Mary River, lat. 26° 30'; long. 152° 30'; and on the Clarke River, a tributary of the Burdekin.

Coal, associated with iron, is abundant from the south boundary to latitude 20° or over 9° of latitude. The principal points where coal is available for shipment, are the Logan River, 27° 40'; the Brisbane River, 27° 30'; the Burrum River, 25° 10'; the Burnett River, 24° 45'; and the Styx River, in Broad Sound, 22° 20'. At present, only the Brisbane River and Burrum River mines are worked on the coast, and the Allora mines, near Warwick.

Diamonds are found in the Stanthorpe District, and on the Burnett River.

Sapphires are frequent in the sands of the water-courses in the Stanthorpe district, and near Rockhampton.

Opals have recently been discovered in considerable numbers on the Barcoo and Bulloo Rivers, in the south-west of the colony.

The productive qualities of the soil of Queensland are fully equal, if not superior, to those of any of the other Australian colonies. Possessing almost every description of soil and climate, it is capable of producing agricultural products peculiar to temperate, semi-tropical, and tropical climes.

The sugar-cane, banana, pine-apple, and other tropical plants, growing luxuriantly in close proximity to cereals, vegetables, and fruits, usually cultivated in Great Britain.

Of late years the cultivation of sugar has sprung up into an established industry of considerable magnitude. The rich scrub and forest lands on the banks of rivers all along the coast, from the southern boundary to lat. 18°, have been found admirably adapted for the cultivation of the sugar-cane. Already, the production of sugar exceeds the local demand, so that sugar has now become an article of export. In 1871, 9,581 acres were under sugar-cane, whilst, for the same year, the quantity of sugar manufactured in the colony amounted to 3,762$\frac{1}{2}$ tons, and the quantity of rum distilled from molasses to 112,979 gallons. As large areas are being annually taken up and planted, the quantities for 1872 will largely exceed those of 1871.

The cultivation of cotton has for several years been established on the coast lands ; the quantity exported in 1871 amounted to 2,603,000 lbs.

Arrowroot is also extensively cultivated and manufactured in the colony ; the quantity exported in 1871 being 40,560 lbs., representing the surplus after supplying the local demand.

A large wheat growing district, a portion of the Darling Downs, lies to the west of the coast range, to which there is ample communication with the coast by railway.

The numbers of live stock in the colony at 31st December, 1871, as given in the Statistical Register of that year, were 91,910 horses, 1,168,235 cattle, 7,403,334 sheep, and 32,707 pigs. At that date there were 107,284,934 acres of waste Crown lands held under 2,214 licenses to depasture live stock, until required for more profitable purposes of settlement.

There are at the present time eight meat preserving establishments in the colony, and the quantity of preserved meat produced in 1871 was 1,775,769 lbs., exclusive of 126,512 lbs. of extract of meat, and these again exclusive of 2,956 tons of tallow. The export of wool for the same year amounted to 22,339,348 lbs.

As will be seen by the specimens of wood collected by Mr. Walter Hill, the Curator of the Botanical Gardens, and more fully described by him in the catalogue, the colony possesses immense wealth in her varied and valuable timbers, both for manufacturing and building purposes.

The Statistics for the past year (1872) not having been compiled, the Commissioners have been obliged to adopt those of 1871; but it will be readily understood, from the circumstance that during the years 1870–1 nearly 155,000 acres of land were alienated from the Crown and settled upon, that with a constantly increasing population, and taking into account the fact that the production of minerals may only be said to have commenced, the exports for 1872 and for the present year will very largely exceed those of 1871.

An exploring party under the leadership of Mr. William Hann, to which Mr. Norman Taylor, late member of the Victoria Geological Survey, was attached, has just returned from an exploration of hitherto unknown country in the York Peninsula. The party penetrated some distance inland north of 14° latitude, and discovered several rivers, on one of which—the Palmer—gold was found for a continuous distance of sixty miles. Strong indications of coal were found over a considerable extent of the territory explored.

Mr. E. Macdonnell, the Government Meteorological Observer, has kindly furnished the following memoranda of the average rainfall and temperature in the south, centre, and north of the colony :—

The rainfall of Queensland may be divided into three classes, viz. :—The coast rains, those falling on the high land from the line formed by the eastern side of the Main Range, and the rains of the interior.

Of the first, records for 13 years have been obtained for Brisbane; but of all the others, the observations have been taken for two or three years only, with the exception of Warwick and Springsure, where records have been preserved for 8 years. The average temperatures of Brisbane and Warwick are given, serving to illustrate that of the most populous districts under cultivation in the south ; but sufficient data has not yet been obtained to permit of the same being done in the northern portions of the colony.

BRISBANE.—Lat., 27° 28′ S.; Long., 153° 6′ E.; distant from coast, 10 miles. Average annual rainfall for 13 years, 51·35 inches, distributed over 122 days. Mean shade temperature for past 6 years, 70·2 degrees. Mean maximum shade, 80 degrees. Mean minimum, 59 degrees. Prevailing winds, north-east.

WARWICK.—Lat., 28° 12′ S.; Long., 152° 16′ E.; distant from coast, 90 miles ; 1,520 feet over sea level. Average annual rainfall for 8 years, 30·85 inches, distributed over 67 days. Mean shade temperature, 66 degrees. Mean maximum shade, 71 degs. Mean minimum, 52 degrees. Prevailing winds, south-east.

SPRINGSURE.—Lat., 24° 10′ S.; Long., 148° E.; distant from coast, 160 miles ; 1,500 feet over sea level. Average annual rainfall for 8 years, 23·36 inches during 47 days.

MACKAY.—Lat., 21° 5′ S.; Long., 149° 5′ E. on coast. Average annual rainfall, 53·18 inches during 101 days.

CARDWELL.—Lat. 18° 6′ S.; Long., 146° E. on coast. Average annual rainfall, 90·47 inches during 116 days.

CATALOGUE OF QUEENSLAND EXHIBITS.

AGRICULTURAL PRODUCTS.

It is a result of the great size and differing climates of Queensland that there is a wide range of agricultural products, for the growth of which our soil and climate are adapted. It is a common, but mistaken, impression that the colony can support nothing but tropical or sub-tropical vegetation, and thus it is popularly called "Banana Land," by the diggers of Victoria and New Zealand, who visit our gold fields. But, as a matter of fact, there is a large area of Queensland, forming the elevated table land or Downs, on and near the summit of the great Dividing Range, where the banana, sugar-cane, or cotton plant, will not flourish, and where the pine-apple, which is grown as a field crop in the low-lying districts, is known only as an imported luxury. The tract of country referred to is proved to be well suited for the growth of wheat, potatoes, and other crops most familiar to the British farmer, and cannot be surpassed elsewhere in the character of its fruits, with the exception of a few descriptions that appear to flourish nowhere out of the United Kingdom and Northern Europe. In the Darling Downs proper, and the extension northwards of that upland tract, there is sufficient land to grow wheat enough to feed our population, however much it may increase. There are at present so many openings for the profitable employment of capital and enterprise, that the principal owners of land on the Darling Downs do not care to incur the trouble and risk of farming; and the greater proportion of the ground is used for the feeding of stock from the natural pasture. The continuance of this state of things is, of course, only a question of time. Pastoral settlement seems to have been, in most countries, the original form of society. A more profitable employment of the soil, where practicable, must follow in its turn; although a large extent of the interior will probably never be employed for anything but for feeding stock, and the pastoral interest will always be a most important one. Along the eastern coast lands of Queensland, agriculture is steadily making its way, and the progress of sugar-growing, especially, has been something that has never before been equalled in the history of industrial advancement. Cotton culti- vation has certainly been influenced by the withdrawal of the bonus granted for a term of years by Parliament, and also from the fact of labor having become scarce and costly, owing to the attractions offered by recent mineral discoveries. This industry, however, cannot fail to advance with the increase of population, as the labor of children can be made available during the picking season.

Farther reference to the different crops grown in Queensland, will be found under their several headings.

CEREALS.

The specimens of Wheat from Darling Downs and East Moreton are not at all equal to some that have been exhibited at local agricultural shows. From causes that have been stated above, the cultivation of this cereal has practically been confined to one district of the colony, and even there it has not taken the place which it will yet assume. It may not be necessary, according to the dicta of political economists, that every country should produce its own bread stuffs; but it is gratifying to know that, should need arise, the soil of Queensland is able to provide the people with "the staff of life." There are flour mills at Brisbane, Warwick, Allora, and Toowoomba; but the work of grinding wheat or other grain, is not sufficient to employ more than a portion of their time. The Queensland flour is, in this colony, better than any that could be imported, for flour always suffers from a sea voyage. From this cause it may not turn out so well when received at London.

There is a good deal of barley grown on the Darling Downs, principally owing to the demand for the grain, for the purpose of malting, that has arisen since the establishment of a brewery at Toowoomba, where the water appears to be peculiarly adapted for the manufacture of malt liquor. Some very good samples have been produced, and the climate and soil appear to be suitable for the growth of this cereal; but the majority of the cultivators require greater experience before they can be completely successful.

Only one sample of maize has been received. It is grown to perfection in every part of the colony where the soil is cultivated, and the farmers probably thought that so common a production was not worth being exhibited.

WHEAT.—1. Mr. R. F. WALKER, Highfields, Darling Downs, Egyptian.

2. Mr. W. TALLOCH, Agricultural Reserve, Warwick, White.

3. Mr. JAMES WILSON, Warwick, White.

> Along with this sample of wheat Mr. Wilson has furnished a statement of the cost of production. From this it appears that on rather less than nineteen acres he raised 800 bushels of wheat, which realised 5s. 6d. per bushel. The whole cost connected with the crop, from ploughing to the final carriage of the grain to market, was £98 12s., giving a net profit of £121 1s.

4. Mr. JOHN DOYLE, Mogill, East Moreton, Red.

> F. J. C. WILDASH, Esquire, Canning Downs, 1 case wheat soil, from Killarney, 20 miles from Warwick.

BARLEY.—5. Mr. R. F. WALKER, Malting.

6. Mr. R. F. WALKER, Bearded.

7 and 8. Mr. R. F. WALKER, Yellow Maize.

FLOUR.—Mr. JAMES KATES, Allora, Darling Downs, Wheaten, 50 lbs.

Mr. WILLIAM PETTIGREW, Wheaten, 20 lbs.

Mr. WILLIAM PETTIGREW, Maizena, 20 lbs.

ARROWROOT, ETC.

This colony appears to be peculiarly suited for the cultivation of Arrowroot, which is gradually supplanting the imported West Indian or Bermuda article in the Australian market. A very small price, perhaps as low as three-pence per pound, would remunerate the grower who manufactures on a large scale, and we may confidently look forward to this valuable alimentary substance occupying an important position amongst our exports. Tapioca and Cassava are also easily produced here, but very little has been done as yet to develop the nascent industry, except on a small scale. The samples exhibited are of fair quality, and the quality will improve when greater experience in the manufacture has been gained.

BOTANIC GARDEN.—

1. West Indian White—*Maranta arundinacea.*
2. East Indian Purple—*Canna edulis.*
3. Brazilian—*Manihot utilissima.*
4. Brazilian Tapioca—*Manihot utilissima.*
5. Brazilian Flour—*Manihot utilissima.*
6. Brazilian Cassava Flour—*Manihot Janipha.*

SUGAR.

At the International Exhibition in 1862 some sugar-canes from Cleveland and the Botanic Gardens were exhibited, and in the Catalogue of the Queensland products, the remark was made:—"There can be but "little doubt that sugar-growing will form one of the "industrial occupations of the country in a few years." This prediction has been more than fulfilled in a shorter period than could well have been anticipated. Sugar-growing is already included among our more prominent industries, and considerable quantities have been shipped to the neighboring colonies, where our sugar has commanded a good price. A refinery has also been established. Queensland, besides providing for its own consumption, will soon be able to supply Australasia with an article of a superior description.

With reference to the exhibits, the particulars of which are given below, it may be explained that they were supplied on application being made to the oldest growers in the different sugar-producing districts.

Along with the samples are given specimens of the soil of the cane-fields in each locality, the latitude and longitude of the latter being stated, in order that an idea may be formed of the extent of the territory in which the cane is successfully cultivated. Sugar being now a leading agricultural product which has started into existence within the last few years, and a large and increasing area of country being taken up for its growth, we may confidently expect that the industry will soon assume very large proportions. The planters have, for the most part, entered without experience on their work, and much has no doubt yet to be learned as to the best mode of cultivation and manufacture adapted to the conditions of our soil and climate. Any suggestion or criticism that the jurors of the International Exhibition, chosen from their practical knowledge of the subject, may be willing to afford, will be regarded with much interest in Queensland.

Messrs. Mackenzie, Brothers, Gairloch, Lower Herbert River.

Situated in Lat. 18° 37'; Long. 146° 10'.
1 bag of Sugar, 56 lbs., marked " 1 A."
1 box of Soil, marked " 1 A."
Made with steam clarifiers, flat battery, Wetzel pan and centrifugal. From Bourbon cane, fourteen months old ; average crop, 2½ tons per acre.

J. E. Davidson, Esq., Alexandra Plantation, Mackay.

Situated in Lat. 21° 11'; Lon. 149° 10'.
3 bags of Sugar, 28 lbs. each.   No. 1, 2, 3, of this year's crop.
No. 1, sample of 240 tons ⎫
No. 2, sample of 120 tons ⎬ Marked " B. 2."
No. 3, sample of 35 tons ⎭
Made up with steam clarifiers, open batteries, Goosden pan and centrifugal, from Bourbon cane.   Crop from 200 acres of land, 395 tons.
1 box of Soil, marked " B. 2."

John Eaton, Esq., Eaton Vale, Maryborough.

Situated in Lat. 25° 38'; Lon. 152° 40'·
1 bag of Sugar, 56 lbs., marked " E. 4."
Made by open process and Wetzel pan, dried in centrifugal.

Messrs. Ramsey Bros, Jindah Estate, Maryborough.

Situated in Lat. 25° 30′ ; Lon. 152° 41′.

1 bag of Sugar, 56 lbs., marked " C. 5."
1 box of Soil, marked " C. 5."

The sample of Sugar is taken from forty tons, made from ten acres of two years' old Bourbon cane, manufactured by the common process, viz., open battery and Wetzel pan.

A. H. Brown, Esq., Antigua Plantation, Maryborough.

Situated in Lat. 25° 50′ ; Lon. 152° 38′.

1 bag of Sugar, 56 lbs., marked " A. 1. Antigua."

Messrs. Raff and Co., Morayfield, Caboolture.

Situated in Lat. 27° 9′ ; Lon. 153° 0′.

1 bag of Sugar, 56 lbs., marked " R. R. 6."
1 box of Soil, marked " R. R. 6."

Made from the black Cheribon cane rattoons. Evaporated in hemispherical pans to density of 20° Reaum., and concentrated in open low temperature pans and centrifugals.

Messrs. James Johnston and Sons, Helenfield, Tingalpa.

Situated in Lat. 27° 30′ ; Lon. 153° 8′.

1 bag of Sugar, 56 lbs., marked " 7, Helenfield."
1 box of Soil, marked " 7, Helenfield."

The sample of Sugar is the produce of four acres of the Chigaco cane, eleven months old, and yielded 1½ tons to the acre, and made by R. M. Johnston. The plant for manufacture is of the commonest description, having cost £1,300 beyond their own labor. It consists of mill, two clarifiers, flat battery of four pans with iron tache and dipper. The liquor is reduced to about 26° Reaum., in the tache, from whence it is skipped into a receiver ; after subsiding a short time it is run into steam-pan, and finished. Said pan is heated by steam coil, the temperature being kept down to about 180° by lathed revolving drum.

The Honorable Louis Hope, Ormiston Plantation, Cleveland.

Situated in Lat. 27° 30′ ; Lon. 153° 16′.

1 bag of Sugar, 56 lbs., marked " L. H. 8."
1 bag of Sugar, 56 lbs., marked " Raw Sugar, L. H. 8."
1 box of Soil, marked " L. H. 8."

Bag No. 8 made from a small Yellow cane, name uncertain (a hairless variety), leaf with smooth edges, third cutting or second ratoons. Bag marked " Raw sugar" from same cane, of first cutting, or plant 23 months old ; steam clarifiers, open battery and Goosden pan—the last a sample from 14 tons off 7 acres of ground ; both from similar soil to that in case, and manured ; both raw sugar dried in centrifugal.

HENRY JORDAN, Esquire, Tygum, Logan River.

Situated in Lat. 27° 45'; Lon. 153° 7'.

1 box of Sugar, 56 lbs., marked " J. 27."
1 box of Soil, marked " J. 27."

The sample of Sugar made from Violet cane, two years old.

The GOVERNMENT PENAL ESTABLISHMENT, St. Helena.

Situated in Lat. 27° 24'; Lon. 153° 15'.

1 bag of Sugar, 56 lbs. marked " broad-arrow."
1 box of Soil, marked " broad-arrow."

Sample of Sugar made from Ribbon cane, 16 months old, yielding two tons to the acre ; boiler, open battery.

Messrs. FRYAR AND STRACHAN, Loganholme, Logan River.

Situated in Lat. 27° 42'; Lon. 153° 14'.

1 bag of Sugar, 56 lbs., marked " S. 10."
1 box of Soil, marked " S. 10."

PHILIP H. NIND, Esquire, Yahwalpa, Pimpama.

Situated in Lat. 27° 48'; Lon. 153° 23'.

1 bag of Sugar, 56 lbs., marked " N. 12."
1 box of Soil, marked " N. 12."

Sample of Sugar made from second ratoons, 18 months old.

ROBERT MUIR, Esquire, Berron, Nerang Creek.

Situated in Lat. 28° 2'; Lon. 153° 25'.

1 bag of Sugar, 56 lbs., marked " M. 11."
1 box of Soil, marked " M. 11."

Sugar made from Ribbon cane rattoons, one year old ; process of manufacture, common open pan battery.

PORT ROYAL MILL, Bald Hills.

Situated in Lat. 27° 19'; Lon. 152° 2'.

1 bag of Sugar, 56 lbs., marked " G. 13."

Sample made from Bourbon cane ; process of manufacture, common open Wetzel pan.

TEA AND COFFEE.

There can be no doubt that both tea and coffee can be cultivated with complete success in Queensland ; but what has been said above as to the range of climate and soil also applies here. In the southern part of the colony it takes some six or seven years to bring the coffee plant to maturity; but further north, in the neighborhood of Port Mackay, Cardwell, &c., it begins to bear in the second year. With regard to tea, it grows luxuriantly on the coast; but the plant, in order to develop the full flavor of the leaf, seems to require the hibernation, or rest for a period, that cannot be had in a climate where the warmth and stimulus to growth is constant. The cultivation and subsequent manufacture connected with the tea and coffee plants require, at certain seasons, a considerable supply of light labor. It may be repeated, what has previously been intimated, that farmers or planters can secure the greatest amount of profit only by cultivating a judicious selection of crops, by which the large amount of labor which any one of them at periods require, may be employed with advantage all the year round.

BOTANIC GARDEN.—

> Coffee, raw, 5 lbs.
>
> Coffee, manufactured, 1 lb.
>
> Tea, manufactured, ½ lb.

TOBACCO.

The exhibits of Tobacco are not so varied in class as they might have been; but are sufficient to prove that a good quality of leaf can be grown in Queensland. Through want of experience in the cultivation of this crop, the farmers do not grow it so much as they would do were they better aware of its profitable nature. Manufacturers state that the Queensland tobacco is inferior to none, but they could not sell it if they offered it as a colonial product; the consequence is, that our local growing goes into the market in the shape of Havannah cigars or cut tobacco of American brands, and meets with ready sale. This very undesirable state of things will, however, alter in the course of time, and Queensland tobacco will, upon its own merits, take a place amongst our material resources.

Mr. K. McLENNAN, Fortitude Valley.—
> 2 cases of manufactured Tobacco (21 lbs. each).
> 1 box of Soil.

Mr. C. CHUBB, Ipswich.—
> 5 lbs. of Virginia-leaf Tobacco.

Mr. HUGH MAHONY, Cunangra, Albert River.—
> 5 lbs. of leaf Tobacco.

Messrs. E. MARWEDEL and Co., Toowoomba.—
> 5 lbs. of leaf Tobacco.

BOTANIC GARDEN.—
> 5 lbs. of Virginia-leaf Tobacco.

WINE.

Only two samples of wine have been forwarded, and, being the produce of last year, it will probably not receive high commendation. There is a large quantity of wine made in the colony, some of which is very good after having the advantage of a year or two in bottle. It is nearly all consumed in the neighborhood where it is produced, and vine growers mostly look for profit from the sale of the fruit. From the great range of soil and climate that we have, it may confidently be anticipated that some of the districts will yet acquire a reputation beyond the colony for their vintages.

WINE.

Messrs. ISAMBERT, Ipswich.—
> 1 case (1 dozen bottles).
> 2 bottles (vintage of 1869).

B

FIBRES.

The increasing demand for fibrous material, in different branches of the industrial arts, has caused a share of attention to be devoted to them for some years past in the Botanic Garden. Queensland is rich in indigenous fibre-yielding plants; and, as time and means permit, valuable discoveries may be made under this head. The work is one pertaining to the objects of the experimental branch of the garden, and is not likely to be taken up by the farmer, who has an ample field for his enterprise in the cultivation of crops known to be remunerative. The Queensland Hemp (*Sida retusa*) is perhaps of greater economic value than the other exhibits enumerated, being an indigenous plant, growing as a weed along the coast districts and making its way gradually into the interior; and, if cultivated, it would form a close and heavy crop, yielding probably as much as a ton of fibre to the acre. With the present appliances, the cost of producing this quantity in a manufactured state, within the colony, is from £30 to £40.

BOTANIC GARDEN.—

1. Queensland Hemp—*Sida retusa*.
2. Queensland Hemp (scutched)—*Sida retusa*.
3. Queensland Rope—*Sida retusa*.
4. Bowstring Hemp—*Sanseveria cylindrica*.
5. Ceylon Hemp—*Sanseveria Zeylanica*.
6. Guinea Hemp—*Sanseveria Guineensis*.
7. Guinea Hemp—*Sanseveria latifolia*.
8. Mexican Hemp—*Furcræa gigantea*.
9. Pete Hemp—*Agava Americana*.
10. Cuba Hemp—*Furcræa Cubensis*.
11. Jute Hemp—*Corchorus capsularis*.
12. Jute and Pete Hemp—*Corchorus olitoris*.
13. Bengal Fibre—*Crotolaria Juncea*.
14. Manilla Hemp—*Musa textilis*.
15. Plantain Hemp—*Musa paradisica*.
16. Rosella Hemp—*Hibiscus sorbifolia*.
17.   —*Hibiscus mutabilis*.
18. Flax—*Linum usitatissimum*.

Mr. A. McPHERSON, Brisbane.—

> 19. Hemp—*Sterculea quadrifina.*

Mr. WEISE, Ipswich.—

> 20. Queensland Hemp—*Sida retusa.*

COTTON.

Only two exhibits of Cotton have been forwarded, and both are of the short-stapled description. A large area of land in the Moreton districts is still taken up in its cultivation, although it is not now so much in favor with the farmers as when a good bonus was paid by the State. When grown in connection with other crops which require an abundant supply of labor at different intervals, such as sugar-cane, tobacco, etc., cotton will still take a much higher position in our productive resources than it has yet done.

G. T. LANG, Brisbane.—

> 1 bag of New Orleans, marked "21."

BOTANIC GARDEN.—

> 1 bag of New Orleans, marked "22."

SILK.

Silk culture has not made much progress, having not yet completely emerged from the stage of experiment. Three samples only have been sent, but there appears lately to have been an increased disposition evinced to embark in this industry. There is everything in its favor here. The mulberry grows luxuriantly, the worms are free from disease, and the climate allows a succession of crops to be obtained during the year.

SILK COCOONS.

Mrs. HINE, Ipswich.—

4 boxes containing four samples, viz. :—Two samples Japanese, two samples East Indian.

The following memoranda were obtained from Mrs. Hine, viz. :—That both the Japanese and the East Indian varieties have gained considerably in weight and strength since she has cultivated them in Queensland. The Japanese, especially for the grain, when first imported some eighteen months ago, produced small puny worms, making cocoons in proportion, whilst at the present time the worms and cocoons have fully doubled their weight. The improvement in the East Indian variety, though not so remarkable, is still very great. The worms usually make their appearance from the grain in the month of July, but owing to severe frost last winter, by which the early leaves of the mulberry trees were destroyed, Mrs. Hine was unable to commence rearing any worms until the beginning of September; the worms previously hatched perished from want of food. In the samples contained in the exhibit, the period occupied from hatching to the time of spinning was about thirty days. The worms were kept in open trays in a room, and fed abundantly on the leaves of the white mulberry (*Morus alba*). The worms were exceedingly healthy during the whole course. The great desideratum is to secure an abundant supply of food, and never allow the worms to want in this respect; again, cleanliness and quiet are essentials, which cannot be too carefully attended to. It does not appear that the variety of mulberry materially affects the health of the worms, or the quality of the silk produced. The chief merit in the white mulberry consists in the larger yield of leaves, the rapid growth, and the impunity with which the trees bear stripping.

In the sample, the worms were hatched in November. The spinning operation was effected in separate paper packets, and when complete, the chrysalis was killed by exposure to the rays of the sun.

Whilst on the subject of silk worms, I would like to offer a remark on the usual mode of transmitting the grain. The complaint is, that a large per centage perishes. This is easily accounted for : the moth, when laying her eggs, deposits them on flat surfaces, and for this purpose sheets of paper or other convenient substances are provided by the cultivator. From these receptacles, the eggs are detached, put up into parcels, and then distributed when wanted for culture. It is, I believe, usual, to slightly gum or size over a paper, and then to sift the grain on it in order that it may adhere to the surface. The eggs of the silk-worm, as well as those of most insects, are provided with a valvular opening on the upper face, through which the larva issues when at maturity. The moth naturally, when depositing her eggs, places them, in simple terms, the right way up. The cultivator, with sized paper, as often as not, effectually fastens his prisoner in its cell, and death is the result. As a naturalist, I would say that the egg ought never to be removed from the place of its deposit by the parent insect.

WILLIAM COOTE, Esq., Rocky Waterholes, Oxley.—

1 case of cocoons.

A. H. GARDNER, Esq., Sandgate.—

1 parcel of cocoons.

DUGONG OIL.

This oil, which is derived from the Halicore Dugong, is used for the same purposes in medicine as cod liver oil, to which it is quite equal as a therapeutic agent, without having the same disagreeable odor. Several years ago it was introduced in Great Britain and the Continent of Europe; the extent of the demand, and the consequent high price secured, induced unscrupulous persons to adulterate the article with common fish oil, owing to which dugong oil, for a time, went out of favor. This unfortunate circumstance might be remedied, were the English importers to purchase only from persons who are above suspicion, and who are in a position to guarantee that the article is genuine.

L. Carmichael, Esquire, Brisbane.—
1 bottle.

MISCELLANEOUS.

In the different regions of this large colony every description of condiment can be produced. The northern coast districts are more favorable to some of the species, but in the southern portion ginger and chilies, from which cayenne pepper is made, grow very freely. Under this heading it may again be said that the development of these, and of many others of our resources, depends entirely upon the settlement of a population on the soil.

A practical chemist, Mr. Carmichael, who has devoted much time and ability to experiments on the vegetable products of Queensland, exhibits some bitters, tinctures, and pomades of novel description, the commercial value of which is at present unknown, but will, no doubt, be pronounced upon by the jurors. Should their verdict be favorable, encouragement will be given for the preparation of a multitude of articles useful in medicine, in the manufacture of perfumes, and in various applications of the arts.

L. CARMICHAEL, Esq., Pharmaceutical Chemist, Brisbane.—

Ayapana Bitters—*Eupatorium ayapana.*
Orange Bitters—*Citrus begaradia.*
Tincture—*Petalostigma quadroculare.*
Tincture—*Alstonia constrica.*
Oil of Lemon—*Citrus lemomum.*
Oil of Orange—*Citrus begaradia.*
Essence of Ginger—*Zingiber officinalis.*
Pomade—*Jasminum grandiflorum.*
Pomade—*Acacia odorata.*

BOTANIC GARDEN.—

Senna Tinnevelly—*Cassia elongata.*
Liquorice, European—*Glycirihiza globra.*

C. CHUBB, Esquire, Ipswich.—

Cayenne Pepper—2 bottles.

BOTANIC GARDEN.—

Allspice—*Pimenta vulgaris.*

BOTANIC GARDEN—FRUITS.—

Queensland Nuts—*Macadamia ternifolia.*
Bunya Bunya—*Araucaria Bedwillii.*

JOHN HALL, Esq., Port Denison.—

Cocoa Nut—*Cocoa nucifera.*
The second that has ripened in Queensland upon a cultivated tree.

THE TIMBERS OF QUEENSLAND.

Owing to the vast area of Queensland, and the diversity of the soil, climate, and altitude of the land, there is a greater variety of indigenous trees than in the rest of the Australian Colonies, and perhaps more than could be found within a similar extent of country in any other part of the world. The specimens of woods are now exhibited from a collection of a few that were easily procured, and were chiefly chosen for their economic value. The list, however, does not include one-fourth of the species that have already been described, and there are most certainly very many which have not yet been classified. Each district of this immense territory is characterised by features in its vegetation peculiar to itself, and years must elapse before all are known and botanically arranged.

It will be for the practical builder, the shipwright, and the cabinet-maker, to pronounce an opinion upon the utility of the woods that have been forwarded; and it is probable that several of them will have a greater value put upon them in the mother country than they receive here. It appears inseparable from the state of affairs in a young colony, that very little time or trouble is devoted to experiment, or to the improvement of existing processes. The same woods that the first settlers made use of, are still employed, as a matter of course, for the same purposes; and timbers, probably of a superior description, are neglected, or used only as firewood. Fortunately, it is different in Queensland from other of the colonies, where some species of forest trees have almost become extinct by destroying them for the sake of the bark, which is used for roofing the ordinary class of dwellings in the bush, and in other ways. However, it is not too soon, even here, to give regard to the expediency of establishing forest reserves in different parts of the colony. In determining the locality of such reserves, assistance will be afforded by the judgment that may be passed in England and Vienna on the specimens of woods now exhibited.

The value of some descriptions of the Australian Eucalypti, for building or railway purposes, has for some time past been fully recognised; and the number of species is greater in Queensland than in other parts of the continent. The case is the same with other woods, the variety of which is very great, that are remarkable for their strength, durability, fineness of grain, or ornamental appearance.

It is impossible to state, at the present period, the price for which all of the Queensland timbers can be placed in the market, for some of which there is no local demand. The cost, when placed on board ship, will not, however, be great, as most of our valuable woods grow on the coast, or the banks of the rivers, or are found within reach of the facilities for transport provided by railway communication.

CONIFERÆ.

1.—ARAUCARIA BIDWILLII, Hook. *Bunya Bunya.* Diameter, 30 to 48 inches; height, 100 to 220 feet.

A noble tree, inhabiting the scrubs in the district between Brisbane and the Burnett Rivers. In the 27th parallel it grows thickly over a portion of country, in extent about 30 miles long and by 12 broad. The tree has a very singular appearance; the trunk is quite straight; its bark is thick and smooth; the branches are produced in whorls of six, seven, or eight; they are horizontal, inflexed, and ascending at the extremities. From the style of growth, singular foliage, and peculiar fresh color, when surrounded with other trees of a different habit and greyish tint, it produces a fine effect, from the striking contrast presented by its rigid growth, and fresh green lance-shaped leaves. The wood is also not only very strong and good, but it is full of beautiful veins, and capable of being polished and worked with the greatest facility. The cones produced on the extreme upper branches, with their apex downwards, are large, measuring 9 to 12 inches in length, and 10 inches in diameter; on coming to maturity they readily shed their seeds, which are 2 to 2½ inches long by 1 inch broad, sweet before being perfectly ripe, and after that resemble roasted chestnuts in taste. In accordance with regulations issued by the Government, the tree is not allowed to be cut down by those who are licensed to fall timber on the Crown lands, the first being used as food by the aboriginals. The trees produce some cones every year, but the principal harvest happens only every three years, when the blacks assemble from all quarters to feast on it. The food seems to have a fattening effect upon them, and they eat large quantities of it, after roasting it at a fire. Contrary to their usual habits, they sometimes store up the Bunya nuts, hiding them in a water-hole for a month or two. Here they germinate, and become offensive in taste to a white man's palate, but are considered by the blacks to have then acquired an improved flavor. The taste of the Bunya when fresh has been described as something between a chestnut and a raw potato.

2.—ARAUCARIA CUNNINGHAMII, Ait. *Moreton Bay Pine.* 36 to 66 ; 150 to 200.

This majestic tree is, without exception, the most ornamental and useful tree in Queensland. Its beautiful regular pyramidal form, and the sombre green of its awl-shaped foliage, command general admiration. It covers immense tracts of land along the coast, and in the interior. It overtops all other trees, whether growing on the alluvial banks near rivers, or upon the steep and rugged mountains in the interior. Its branches are produced in whorls from six to eight, horizontally and spreading. The bark is thick and brownish. The timber is an article of great commercial importance, and is used extensively in this colony. The wood is strong and durable when kept dry, but soon decays when exposed to alternate damp and dry. When procured from the mountains in the interior it is fine-grained, and is susceptible of a high polish, which excels that of satinwood or bird's-eye maple. The resin which exudes is very remarkable ; it has all the transparency and whiteness of crystal, and that portion of it which adheres to the trees hangs from them in shape of icicles, which are sometimes 3 feet long, and 6 to 12 inches broad. The sawyers receive at the present time 65s. to 70s. per 1,000 feet, some trees yielding as much as 10,000 of saleable timber.

3.—DAMMARA ROBUSTA, Moore. *Kawrie or Dundathu Pine.* 36 to 72 ; 80 to 130.

This huge tree inhabits the alluvial banks on the rivers near the coast in the Wide Bay District. It has a smooth-barked trunk, of a lead color ; the branches are produced in whorls from 5 to 10, distant, spreading, and of a large size. The wood is fine-grained, free of knots, and easily worked. It is, however, not a plentiful tree. At the present time the sawyers are receiving 90s. per 1,000 feet.

4.—CALLITRIS COLUMNARIS, F. M. *Cypress Pine.* 20 to 30 ; 40 to 60.

This tree forms vast tracts along the coast, growing on barran sandy soils. Its form is pyramidal, and of great beauty ; the trunk has a brownish ridgy bark, the branches are numerous and ascending. The timber is an article of great importance, and is receiving that attention that it deserves from the timber merchants. The wood is durable, fine-grained, fragrant, and capable of a high polish. It is used for piles of wharves, and for sheathing punts and boats—it resists the attacks of cobra and white ants; the root is valued by cabinet-makers for veneering purposes. The present time sawyers are getting 80s. per 1,000 feet.

5.—CALLITRIS VERRUCOSA, R. B. *The Desert Cypress Pine.* 12 to 24; 50 to 70.

A handsome tree, more or less scattered through the sandy ridges in the Darling Downs District. The timber is much used by some of the settlers for building purposes.

6.—CALLITRIS ENDLICHERI, Parl. *The Mountain Cypress Pine.* 9 to 18; 40 to 50.

A middle-sized tree, found on rocky and not densely timbered ranges, bordering on the Logan and Albert Rivers.

7.—PODOCARPUS ELATUS, R. B. *She Pine.* 20 to 36; 50 to 80.

A very beautiful tree, with elongated trunk, rarely cylindrical; wood free from knots, soft, close, easily worked; good for joiner's work. It occurs very frequently in the scrubs along the coast.

AMENTACEÆ.

8.—CASUARINA TENUISSIMA, Sieb. *River Oak.* 18 to 22; 40 to 70.

A beautiful picturesque tree, growing only in or near the borders of rivers or creeks; its wood strong, tough, and occasionally used for staves and shingles.

9.—CASUARINA LEPTOCLADA, Miq. *The Erect Sheoak.* 9 to 15; 20 to 30.

A small tree, forming small thickets in open forest ground; wood close, prettily marked, but not durable.

10.—CASUARINA EQUISETIFOLIA, Frost. *Swamp Oak.* 12 to 20; 50 to 70.

This species is found growing in great abundance near salt-water marshes or inlets; the wood is close-grained, and beautifully marked, and is used for purposes in which lightness and toughness are required.

11.—Casuarina torulosa, Ait. *Forest Oak*, Beefwood. 9 to 15; 30 to 35.

A small tree occupying large tracts of land in the open forest; the timber is much used for fuel; the wood is close and prettily marked, yielding handsome veneers.

212.—Casuarina Cunninghamii, Miq. *Fire Oak.* 6 to 10; 20 to 30.

A small tree found in the Brigalow scrubs; wood not much used except for fuel.

MELEACEÆ.

12.—Cedrela Toona, Rox. *Red Cedar.* 24 to 76; 100 to 150.

This magnificent deciduous tree is found in scrubs along the coast, and occasionally extending inland for a considerable distance; the trunk is erect and massive, covered with a rough scaly brown bark, which, in the young branches, is of a grey color; the branches have an upward tendency, and have a very graceful appearance. In favorable situations, where it has room to spread, it puts out large branches, the junctions of which with the stem, furnish those beautiful curled pieces of which the choicest veneers are made; the timber is an article of great commercial importance, and extensively exported to other colonies. At the present time the sawyers are receiving 180 shillings to 200 shillings per thousand feet.

13.—Flindersia Australis, R. B. *Flindosa.* 36 to 48; 80 to 100.

A robust tree of general occurrence in the scrubs on the banks of rivers; the trunk is of a good size, covered with a smooth, scaly, lead-colored bark; the branches thick, tortuous, and numerous; the wood is hard, close, and of great strength and durability; it has long been known to the timber merchants as being a very hard timber and difficult to cut up with the saw; for that reason little attention has been paid to procuring it.

14.—Flindersia Oxleyana, F. M. *Light-yellow wood.* 24 to 42; 80 to 100.

This fine tree is found in the same situations as the red cedar. It has a beautiful symmetrical trunk, which, towards the upper part, throws out many branches; the head is conical, and occupies about one-thirtieth part of the stem. The wood is strong, durable, and fine-grained, and on that account capable of a high polish. It could be applied to the same purpose as the cedar. It is further valuable for its dyeing properties. At the present time the sawyers are receiving at the rate of 80 shillings per thousand feet.

15.—FLINDERSIA BENNETIANA, F. M. *Bogum Bogum.*
    18 to 26; 70 to 90.

A large smooth-stemmed tree; timber close-grained, which is seldom used. It splits well; might, probably, be valuable for staves.

16.—FLINDERSIA MAMULOSA, F. M. *Spotted Tree of the Colonists.* 12 to 18; 30 to 40.

A middle-sized tree; the trunk spotted by the falling off of the outer bark in patches; timber close-grained, and said to be durable; rather plentiful in the rosewood scrubs in the Darling Downs District.

17.—OWENIA VENOSA, F. M. *Sour Plum.* 12 to 24; 40 to 65.

A moderate-sized shady tree, common in the Brigalow scrubs in the Darling Downs District. Wood of a rose color. Its great strength renders it fit for many purposes.

18.—OWENIA CERASIFERA, F. M. *Sweet Plum.* 9 to 18; 25 to 35.

A small, but a very beautiful tree, with fine dark-green glossy foliage; wood hard, and of a dark-red color, finely marked, and takes a very high polish.

19.—AMOORA NITEDULA, Benth.
    18 to 30; 70 to 90.

A large-sized tree, of frequent occurrence in scrubs bordering the coast. Timber not of much importance.

20.—SYNOUM GLANDULOSUM, A. Juss.
    15 to 24; 35 to 60.

A moderate-sized tree, of very general occurrence in many places. Timber firm and easily worked.

21.—DYSOXYLON MUELLERI, Benth. *Pencil Cedar.*
    20 to 35; 70 to 90.

A large-sized tree, with a bright-green foliage, inhabiting the rich alluvial flats upon the banks of the rivers in the districts of Moreton Bay and Wide Bay. Wood of a red color, used for cabinet purposes and indoor work. When fresh cut, the timber has much the smell of a Swedish turnip.

215.—Dysoxylon rufum, Benth. *Bastard Cedar Pencil Wood.* 20 to 24; 40 to 60.

A moderate-sized tree, occurring in many of the scrubs on the coast, and also in the interior. Wood is nicely grained, and used for various purposes, but principally for cabinet work, for turning, &c.

23.—Melia composita, Willd. 15 to 20; 50 to 60.

A middle-sized deciduous tree, ranging never far away from the coast. Wood soft, and not considered to be of much value.

SIMARUBEÆ.

24.—Ailanthus imberbiflora, F. M. 20 to 28; 50 to 70.

A large tree, having a lofty cylindrical stem; found in the coast scrubs. Wood light, soft, and appears to be of little durability.

RUTACEÆ.

25.—Bosistoa sapindiformis, F. M. 6 to 12; 15 to 20.

A small but very handsome tree, abounding in most of the scrubs near the sources of the Logan and Albert Rivers. Wood close and light.

26.—Citrus Australis, Planch. *Native Orange.* 6 to 14.

This small and handsome tree grows in abundance in the borders of scrubs both on the coast and in the interior. The trunk is erect, with many diffused branches armed with axillary straight thorns of about half an inch long. The fruit is about one and a-half inches in diameter, almost globular; an agreeable beverage is produced from its acid juice. The wood is hard, close-grained, and of a fine light-yellow color.

27.—Citrus Australasica, F. M. *Native Lime.* 6 to 10; 15 to 20.

A low-sized and beautiful tree, growing in the scrubs on the Brisbane and Pine Rivers. The trunk is erect and well diffused, with small branches bearing fruit about two inches long, and of an oblong form. The wood is close-grained, hard, and of a yellow color.

28.—ATALANTIA GLAUCA, Hook. *The Native Cumquat.* 2 to 6; 8 to 15.

A small tree or shrub, armed with straight or incurved axillary spines of a quarter of an inch long upon the branches. The fruit is globular, about half of an inch in diameter, and produces an agreeable beverage from its acid juice. The wood is close-grained, and takes a fine polish. Found in great abundance in the Darling Downs and the Maranoa districts.

29.—ACRONYCHIA BAUERI, Schott. 6 to 12; 16 to 24.

A small-sized but beautiful tree, found in great abundance in most of the scrubs bordering the coast. Wood close-grained, but not used.

30.—ACRONYCHIA IMPERFORATA, F. M. 12 to 20; 20 to 40.

A middle-sized tree, occurring in the scrubs bordering the Brisbane River. The timber is fine-grained, easily worked, but not much used.

31.—ACRONYCHIA LÆVIS, Frost. 15 to 20; 30 to 50.

A tall slender tree; timber not used.

221.—PENTACERAS AUSTRALIS, Hook. *White Cedar of the Colonists.* 12 to 20; 40 to 60.

A very handsome moderate tree; occurs principally in the scrubs near the coast. The wood is close-grained, tough, and firm, but as yet not much used.

32.—ZANTHOXYLON BRACHYACANTHUM, F. M. *Satin Wood.* 6 to 9; 20 to 30.

This slender prickly tree is found in small quantities in most of the scrubs in Queensland. The wood is close-grained and of a yellow color, and is susceptible of high polish.

33.—GEIJERA PARVIFLORA, Lindl. 6 to 12; 20 to 30.

A small-sized but beautiful tree of a weeping habit, occurring in many of the Brigalow scrubs. Timber hard, close-grained, which, however, splits in seasoning.

34.—GEIJERA MUELLERI, Benth. *Balsam Capivi Tree.* 12 to 18; 40 to 60.

A moderate-sized tree, conspicuous for its smooth shining leaves. Dispersed through the Araucaria scrubs around Ipswich. The wood is nicely marked, and of agreeable fragrance when green; not yet used.

35.—Evadia Micrococca, F. M.
6 to 10; 20 to 30.

A small-sized tree of no great beauty; met with in the scrubs on the banks of rivers in the Moreton Bay District.

CELASTRINEÆ.
36.—Celastrus dispermus, F. M.
3 to 5; 12 to 16.

A small-size tree of some beauty when not over crowded with other trees. Wood close-grained, and takes a fine polish.

182.—Siphonodon Australe, Benth.
12 to 24; 40 to 60.

A handsome scrub tree of frequent occurrence. Wood close-grained, of a yellowish color.

38.—Denhamia pittosporoides, F. M.
6 to 8; 20 to 30.

A slender-growing tree; growing on the borders of scrubs inland from the coast; the timber is hard, fine-grained, and takes a good polish.

39.—Denhamia obscura, Meisn.
3 to 5; 12 to 20.

A tall shrub—a small tree; in the Brigalow scrubs near Ipswich. Wood fine-grained and tough.

40.—Elæodendron Australe, Vent.
4 to 12; 20 to 30.

A slender-growing tree. Wood close-grained and prettily marked.

RHAMNEÆ.
41.—Alphitonia excelsa, Reissek. *Mountain or Red Ash.* 18 to 24; 45 to 60.

This valuable tree is found plentiful in the forest and in the scrubs, both on the coast and in the interior. The wood is hard, close-grained, durable, and will take a high polish; it is also suitable for gun stocks, and for a variety of other purposes.

PITTOSPOREÆ.

42.—PITTOSPORUM RHOMBIFOLIUM, A. Cunn.
6 to 12; 40 to 55.

A fine tree, with fine glossy foliage; scrubs on the Brisbane River. The wood is of a white color; not used.

43.—PITTOSPORUM BICOLOR, Hook.
6 to 12; 20 to 40.

A small but graceful weeping tree; in the more open forest ground in the West Moreton and Darling Downs districts. Timber close-grained.

44.—PITTOSPORUM PHILLYRŒOIDES, D. C.
4 to 6; 20 to 35.

A small tree; met with in many of the Brigalow scrubs. Wood close-grained, and of a white color.

CAPPARIDEÆ.

45.—CAPPRIS NOBILIS, F. M. *Small Native Pomegranate.* 6 to 14; 20 to 35.

A small tree, of great beauty when in blossom. The wood is hard, and close-grained.

46.—CAPPRIS MITCHELLI, Lindl. *Wild Native Pomegranate.* 10 to 12; 14 to 30.

Handsome small tree; in the Brigalow scrubs in the Darling Downs district. The timber is hard, and close-grained.

47.—APOPYLLUM ANOMALUM, F. M.
6 to 10; 20 to 30.

A shrub or tree, almost leafless, with cylindrical, often pendulous, branches; occurring in the Bigalow scrubs in the Darling Downs District. Wood very hard.

STERCULIACEÆ.

48.—STERCULIA QUADRIFIDA, R. B.
18 to 24; 40 to 60.

A moderate-sized deciduous tree. Wood soft and spongy; the bark used for nets and fishing-lines.

49.—Sterculia diversifolia, G. Don.
18 to 24 ; 50 to 60.

This is a very handsome tree ; in many of the coast and the scrubs in the interior. Timber soft and of no value.

50.—Sterculia lurida, F. M.
12 to 15 ; 40 to 50.

A very beautiful tree in appearance. Timber not used.

51.—Tarrietia argyrodendron, Benth. *Silver Tree.*
24 to 34 ; 70 to 90.

A large tree, with magnificent canopy of silvery foliage ; growing in great quantities in the scrubs bordering the banks of the river. The timber is not much used at present.

52.—Tarrietia actinodendron, F. M. 18 to 30 ; 60 to 70.

This tree is plentiful in the coast scrubs. It is remarkable for being umbrageous and graceful in its appearance ; the timber is tough and close grained, but seldom used.

53.—Commersonia echinata, Frost. 6 to 12 ; 20 to 30.

A tall shrub or small tree, of general occurrence on the banks of rivers ; the aboriginals use the fibre of the bark for kangaroo and fishing nets ; timber not used.

LINEÆ.

54.—Erythroxylon Australe, F. M. 6 to 12 ; 20 to 30.

This shrub or small-sized tree occurs in considerable abundance in the Brigalow scrub near Ipswich ; wood hard, fine-grained, it takes a good polish, and can be used for cabinet work.

SAPINDACEÆ.

55.—Cupania xylocarpa, A. Cunn. 12 to 24 ; 40 to 60.

A moderate-sized tree in good situations ; timber close-grained and hard, particularly so when dry. Not used.

56.—Cupania serrata, F. M. 8 to 14 ; 20 to 30.

A very ornamental tree of small size, plentiful in the scrubs on the banks of rivers ; timber close-grained. Not used.

C

57.—DIPLOYLOTTIS CUNNINGHAMII, Hook. *Native Tamarind,* 12 to 20 ; 40 to 55.

This elegant-growing tree, with its large pinnate leaves, producing every year large racemes of beautiful acid fruit, used for preserves by the colonists. Timber, although compact and durable, seldom used.

58.—CUPANIA SEMIGLAUCA,. F. M. 10 to 20 ; 30 to 60.

A middle-sized tree. Wood soft, and as yet of no recognised value.

59.—CUPANIA ANACARDIOIDES, F. M. 12 to 18 ; 30 to 40.

A slender tree, in considerable abundance on the alluvial banks of rivers. Timber seldom used.

60.—CUPANIA PSEUDORHUS, A. R. 14 to 20 ; 30 to 50.

A spreading tree of moderate size, growing in great abundance in the scrubs bordering the coast. Wood fine-grained and beautiful.

61.—RATONIA PYRIFORMIS, Benth. 10 to 18 ; 30 to 45.

A handsome moderate-sized tree ; with large glossy pinnate leaves. Wood firm, close-grained.

62.—NEPHELIUM TOMENTOSUM, F. M. 10 to 15 ; 30 to 40.

A small-sized tree. Timber not used.

63.—HETERODENDRON OLEÆFOLIUM, Desf. 4 to 10 ; 20 to 30.

A tall shrub or small tree, occurring in some abundance in the Brigalow scrubs near Ipswich, and the Gowrie scrub. Wood hard, close-grained, and capable of a high polish.

64.—HETERODENDRON DIVERSIFOLIUM, F. M. 4 to 6 ; 10 to 15.

Handsome shrub, common in Brigalow scrubs. Wood of a reddish color ; its great strength renders it fit for pick-handles.

67.—HARPULLA PENDULA, Planch. *Tulip Wood.* 14 to 24 ; 50 to 60.

A very beautiful-growing tree, with glossy green pinnate leaves ; found in some abundance on the alluvial banks of rivers. The wood is close-grained, firm, and beautifully marked ; much esteemed for cabinet work.

68.—DODONÆA TRIQUETRA, Andr. *Hop Bush.* 3 to 4 ; 10 to 12.

Branching shrub. Wood hard, close-grained.

ANACARDIACEÆ.

69.—RHUS RHODANTHEMIA, F. M. *Dark Yellow-wood.*
18 to 24; 50 to 70.

A picturesque tree, of general occurrence in the scrubs on the banks of rivers; the trunk is of moderate size, covered with a rough scaly bark; the branches are small and numerous, the leaves are pinnate, the flowers are red. The wood is soft, fine-grained, and beautifully marked, and is much esteemed for cabinet work. At the present time the sawyers are receiving 100 shillings per thousand feet.

70.—SPONDEAS SOLANDRI, Benth. 24 to 36; 40 to 60.

A moderate-sized tree of rare occurrance in the coast scrubs. Wood soft when cut, but afterwards becomes hard and tough; not as yet used.

ARALIACEÆ.

71.—PANAX ELEGANS, F. M. 12 to 16; 30 to 40.

A singular, moderate tree, with magnificent, large, simple, or doubly pinnate leaves, occurring in dense scrubs. Wood light, soft, and of little durability.

RUBIACEÆ.

72.—SARCOCEPHALUS CORDATUS, Miq. *Leichhardt's Tree.*
24 to 30; 40 to 60.

A handsome and beautiful moderate-sized tree, found on the alluvial banks of the Don River, Port Denison, &c., &c. Its wood is soft, close-grained, and takes a good polish; often used for building and other purposes.

73.—IXORA PAVETTA, ROX.
2 to 4; 8 to 10.

A beautiful flowering shrub found in the borders of scrubs; wood very hard and fine grained.

74.—HODGKINSONIA OVALIFLORA, F. M.
6 to 10; 12 to 20.

Small slender tree; wood close grained.

75.—CANTHIUM LUCIDUM, Hook and Arn.
6 to 12; 20 to 30.

Small tree; wood hard and close grained.

76.—Canthium oleifolium, Hook.
4 to 10 ; 25 to 30.

In Brigalow scrubs, near Ipswich. A tall shrub, or small tree of a beautiful habit ; wood hard, close-grained, and capable of a high polish.

77.—Canthium latifolium, R. B.
8 to 12 ; 25 to 30.

A small tree, with very close-grained hard wood; when seasoned carefully is excellent for turnery, and promises to be good for wood engraving.

78.—Canthium vacciniifolium, F. M.
2 to 4 ; 6 to 10.

Handsome shrub; wood close-grained.

79.—Canthium coprosmoides, F. M.
4 to 6 ; 20 to 30.

A slender-growing shrub, or small tree, with close-grained wood. Not yet used.

80.—Canthium attenuatum, R. B.
3 to 6 ; 15 to 20.

A beautiful shrub; wood close-grained.

81.—Same as No. 78.

82.—Cœlospermum paniculatum, F. M.
3 to 5 ; 100 to 150.

A robust woody climber; wood soft and finely grained ; frequent in moist low scrubs.

MYRTACEÆ.

83.—Leptospermum flavescens, Sm.
3 to 6 ; 10 to 15.

A tall shrub about fresh-water creeks, and wood hard and close-grained.

86.—Callistemon lanceolatus, D. C. *Bottle-brush Tree.* 12 to 18 ; 30 to 40.

A small branching tree, growing in or near the beds of rivers ; wood hard, heavy.

87.—CALISTEMON SALIGNUS, D. C. *Broad-leaved Tea Tree.* 18 to 24; 40 to 60.

Handsome tree when in flower; wood very hard and close-grained; apt to split in drying; it has the reputation of being very durable under ground. The outer bark can easily be detached in innumerable thin layers, very soft to the touch.

88.—MELALUCA GENISTIFOLIA, Sm. 6 to 12; 30 to 40.

Small tree; wood hard, close-grained. Not used.

89.—MELALUCA LEUCADENDRON, Lin. *White Tea Tree.* 24 to 40; 40 to 60.

A moderate-sized tree, with a thick spongy bark, peeling off in layers : the timber is hard and close-grained; excellent for posts in damp places; said to be almost imperishable under ground.

90.—MELALUCA STYPHELIOIDES, Sm. *Prickly-leaved Tea Tree.* 24 to 30; 40 to 60.

A moderate-sized tree; the timber is very hard, close-grained; stands well in damp situations. It is said that this timber has never been known to decay.

84.—MELALUCA LINARIIFOLIA, Sm. 20 to 24; 30 to 40.

A small-sized tree; wood close-grained, hard, and durable.

85.—MELALUCA NODOSA, Sm. *Tea Tree.* 10 to 20; 30 to 40.

A small tree; timber and bark very like those of the preceding two species.

92.—ANGOPHORA SUBVELUTINA, F. M. *Apple-tree.* 20 to 26; 40 to 60.

A large wide-spreading tree, with rough persistent bark; occurring generally on rich forest lands; timber strong and durable, often used by wheelwrights.

93.—EUCALYPTUS PILULARIS, Sm. *Black-butt.* 24 to 40; 60 to 80.

A moderate-sized or large tree, with dark-colored rough bark at the base, smooth and falling off in flakes upwards and on the branches; furnishes excellent timber for house carpentry, or any purpose where strength and durability are required; at the present time the sawyers are receiving at the rate of 80s. to 90s. per thousand feet.

94.—EUCALYPTUS HŒMASTOMA, S. M. *Spotted Gum.* 24 to 48 ; 60 to 90.

A large tree, with a smooth deciduous bark leaving the trunk spotted or varigated where it falls off; considered a first-class timber for ship building, and much used for wheelwright's work, and other purposes.

95.—EUCALYPTUS MICROCORYS, F. M. 18 to 30 ; 60 to 80.

A tall tree with a persistent furrowed fibrous bark, occurring in the forest, grown near the Brisbane River; timber used by wheelwrights for naves, felloes, and spokes.

96.—EUCALYPTUS HEMIPHLOIA, F. M. *Yellow Box.* 20 to 30 ; 40 to 60.

A moderate-sized tree, producing an excellent timber, famous for its hardness, toughness, and durability.

97.—EUCALYPTUS SIDEROPHLOIA, Benth. *Ironbark.* 20 to 30 ; 60 to 80.

A large tree, with a straight even bole, and a hard, persistent, rough-furrowed bark ; the timber is of the highest reputation for strength and durability, and is very much used for large beams in building stores for heavy goods, railway bridges, sleepers, and other purposes where great strength is required ; occupant of many ridgy, stony, forest grounds throughout the districts of East and West Moreton, and the Darling Downs districts ; and at the present time the sawyers are receiving at the rate of 70s. to 80s. per thousand feet.

98.—EUCALYPTUS MELANOPHLOIA, F. M. *Silver-leaved Ironbark.* 18 to 20 ; 30 to 60.

A middle-sized tree, with a blackish, persistent, deeply-furrowed bark ; occurring generally on open forest ground, in some situations where the soil is of a first-class description for cultivation. The timber is hard, tough, and durable.

99.—EUCALYPTUS MACULATA, Hook. *Spotted Gum.* 20 to 30 ; 60 to 80.

A large-sized tree, with a smooth bark falling off in patches, so as to give the trunk a spotted appearance ; timber highly prized in some localities for ordinary purposes.

100.—EUCALYPTUS SALIGNA, Sm. *Grey Gum.* 24 to 34; 60 to 80.

A tree usually of a large size; it is characterized by a smooth, silver-grey, shining bark, shedding in thin longitudinal strips; timber in good repute for various purposes. Of frequent occurrence on the forest ridges near the Brisbane River.

101.—EUCALYPTUS RESINFERA, Sm. *Red Mahogany.* 20 to 30; 60 to 70.

A good-sized tree, with a rough persistent bark on the trunk, but more or less deciduous on the branches; timber much prized for its strength and durability. Found in the valley near Mogill.

102.—EUCALYPTUS CORYMBOSA, Sm. *Bloodwood.* 24 to 30; 50 to 60.

A fair-sized tree, timber subject to gum veins, but its wood is in good repute for durability. It is much used for post and rails. It is of common occurrence.

103.—EUCALYPTUS BOTRYOIDES, Sm. *Blue Gum.* 30 to 48; 70 to 90.

A tall handsome tree, of frequent occurrence both upon the coast and in the interior. A very valuable timber, hard, tough, and durable, excellent for naves and felloes of wheels, and for work underground. At the present time the sawyers are receiving 75s. per thousand feet.

104.—EUCALYPTUS TERETICORNIS, Sm. *Red Gum.* 18 to 30; 60 to 80.

A moderate-sized tree, with a smooth ash-colored bark; timber much used in fencing, building, plough beams, poles and shafts of drays; found in rich alluvial flats.

105.—EUCALYPTUS STUARTIANA, F. M. *Turpentine Tree.* 24 to 36; 60 to 80.

This species—with its large, huge branches, the bark of which is smooth and deciduous, that of the trunk rough and rigid and somewhat stringy—is of common occurrence; the timber is hard, and said to be exceedingly durable under ground; it is difficult to burn.

106.—EUCALYPTUS FIBROSA, F. M. *Stringy Bark.* 18 to 24; 40 to 60.

A species yielding timber much prized for flooring boards, of considerable strength and durability.

108.—EUCALYPTUS TESSELARIS, F. M. *Moreton Bay Ash.*
14 to 24; 30 to 60.

A middle-sized tree ; the bark on the lower portion of the trunk dark-colored, persistent, and splitting into numerous angular pieces ; the bark on remainder of the trunk and branches is smooth and ash-colored, falling off in the spring and early summer months in thin sheets ; timber brownish, not hard, but tough.

109.—BACKHOUSIA MYRTIFOLIA, Hook and Harv.
Myrtle. 12 to 18 ; 20 to 40.

Small tree, with very branching head and dark-green foliage ; wood close-grained and prettily marked.

167.—BACKHOUSIA CITRIODORA, F. M.
6 to 12 ; 30 to 30.

A small-sized tree ; the wood is hard, fine-grained, and likely to be useful for several purposes.

165.—MYRTUS ACMENIOIDES, F. M.
12 to 18 ; 30 to 40.

A small tree of considerable beauty, frequent in the scrubs ; wood close-grained. Not much known.

168.—EUGENIA SMITHII, Poir. *Lilly Pillies.* 12 to 18 ;
30 to 40.

A beautiful tree, with dense foliage, producing a profusion of fruit, very acid, but eatable and wholesome. Wood close, apt to rend in drying.

169.—EUGENA VENTENETII, Benth.
18 to 20 ; 40 to 60.

A handsome tree, of frequent occurrence in the moist scrubs, its fine glossy leaves being densely clustered together at the ends of the long slender branches. Wood close-grained, and of a pinkish hue.

111.—MYRTUS HILLII, Benth. *Scrub Ironwood.* 6 to
12 ; 20 to 40.

A small-sized tree, frequent in low moist scrubs. Wood remarkably hard.

110.—RHODAMNIA TRINERIRA, Blum.
10 to 18 ; 20 to 30.

Small tree, beautiful when in flower. Wood close-grained and firm.

112.—Rhodomyrtus psidioides, Benth.
12 to 20 ; 30 to 40.

A tree of considerable beauty, frequent in scrubs. Wood close-grained ; not much known.

113.—Rhodamnia argenta, Benth.
15 to 22 ; 40 to 60.

A tall tree, found in great abundance in the moist low scrubs along the coast. Wood tough and firm.

114.—Tristania conferta, R. B. *Box.* 36 to 50 ; 80 to 100.

A fine-looking tree, with a smooth brown deciduous bark and dense foliage ; very generally distributed on open forest ground. Its timber is much prized for its strength and durable qualities.

116.—Barringtonia carya, F. M. *Broad - leaved Apple-tree.* 14 to 20 ; 40 to 50.

A graceful tree, with broad leaves and handsome pink and white flowers ; found generally in rich alluvial soils on the banks of the Burdekin River, &c. Wood soft when cut, and of a blood-red color towards the centre.

PROTEACEÆ.

110*.—Grevellia robusta. *Silky Oak.* 30 to 40 ; 80 to 100.

A lofty tree, of frequent occurrence in the scrubs along the coast, and for a considerable distance in the interior. The wood is extensively used for staves for tallow casks and is much in repute for cabinet work. At the present the sawyers are receiving at the rate of 80s. to 90s. per thousand feet.

111*.—Stenocarpus sinuatus, Endl. *Tulip Tree.* 18 to 30 ; 40 to 80.

A charming, moderate-sized tree, with dense, bright, glossy foliage. It occurs often in scrubs, some distance from the coast. The wood is nicely marked, and would admit of a good polish.

112*.—Macadamia ternifolia, F. M. *Queensland Nut.* 3 to 12 ; 30 to 50.

A small-sized tree with a very dense foliage. Found in dense, moist scrubs on the banks of rivers ; wood firm, fine-grained, and takes a good polish. This tree bears an edible nut of excellent flavor, which is relished by the white colonists as well as by the aborigines. It forms a nutritious article of food to the latter, and, in consequence, the same restriction with regard to this tree, as in the case of *Araucaria Bedwillii* (Bunya Bunya), is made in the licenses issued for cutting timber.

113*.—ORITES EXCELSA, R. B.
6 to 14 ; 30 to 60.

A handsome tree, of frequent occurrence in the scrubs bordering the coast; timber hard, nicely marked, and takes a good polish.

114*.—BANKSIA INTEGRIFOLIA, Linn. *Beef Wood.* 8 to 12 ; 20 to 30.

A low branching tree, occurring very frequent on sandy ridges near the coast, and for a considerable distance in the interior. Wood nicely marked.

115*.—PERSOONIA LUCIDA, VAR. LATIFOLIA, ·A. Cunn.
3 to 7 ; 10 to 20.

A small-sized tree, with a lamellose bark, found in sandy ridges on the coast. Wood prettily marked, but not durable.

116*.—GREVELLIA HILLIANA, F. M.
10 to 18 ; 40 to 60.

A beautiful tree, found in thick scrubs on the banks of the Logan and Albert Rivers. Wood easily wrought ; not used.

216.—GREVELLIA GIBBOSA, R. B.
8 to 12 ; 20 to 30.

A small tree, occurring in the forest ground on the bank of the Don River. Wood fine-grained and nicely marked.

RHIZOPHOREÆ.

116*2.—BRUGUIERA RHEEDII, Blume. *Mangrove.* 6 to 12 ; 12 to 20.

Small tree. Wood very pretty ; the bark is stringent, and is used for tanning purposes.

THYMELACEÆ.

117.—EXOCARPUS LATIFOLIUS, R. B. *Broad-leaved Cherry-tree.* 6 to 9 ; 12 to 25.

A beautiful, small, slender tree, with scaly black-colored bark ; of frequent occurrence in the scrubs on the coast, as well as a considerable distance in the interior ; the wood is very hard and fragrant, excellent for cabinet work.

118.—Exocarpus cupressiformus, R. B. *Cherry-tree*, 4 to 8; 10 to 16.

A small tree with spreading loose habit of growth. It is found sparingly upon the open forest grounds; the wood is close-grained and promises to be handsome.

SANTALACEÆ.

119.—Santalum lanceolatum, R. B. *Sandal Wood*. 3 to 6; 15 to 25.

A small tree sparingly distributed through the Brigalow scrubs; the wood is close-grained, and takes a good polish.

MYOPORINEÆ.

120.—Eromophylla Mitchelli, Benth. *Bastard Sandal Wood.* 6 to 12; 20 to 30.

A small tree of frequent occurrence in open forest land in the Darling Downs District; the wood is very hard, beautifully grained and very fragrant; it will turn out handsome veneers for cabinet work.

124.—Myoporum acumenatum, Var. parviflorum, R. B. 4 to 6; 12 to 15.

Timber soft and light.

125.—Myoporum acumenatum, R. B. 6 to 14; 15 to 25.

A small-sized tree found on the borders of low moist scrubs; wood soft and of little value.

126.—Myoporum platycarpum, R. B. 12 to 15; 15 to 25.

A small tree, wood close-grained, not yet used.

VERBENACEÆ.

121.—Avicennia officinalis, Linn. *Mangrove.* 19 to 20; 20 to 30.

A low branching tree, found on salt-water estuaries; its wood, when small, is valued for stonemasons' mallets, and is used for knees of boats and vessels; the ashes are used in soap manufacture.

122.—Gmelina Leichhardtii, F. M. *Beech*. 24 to 36; 80 to 100.

This very useful tree has a lofty cylindrical stem, the bark ash-colored, the leaves ovate, downy underneath, from four to six inches long, and from two to three wide; the wood has, by experience, been found to be very useful. It is easily worked, and, at the same time, is both strong and durable; it does not expand by damp, and contract by dry weather. It is found in small quantities in the scrubs bordering the rivers on the coast. At the present time the sawyers are receiving at the rate of 180s. to 200s. per thousand feet.

123.—Vitex lignum vitæ, A. Cunn. *Scrub Lignum Vitæ*. 20 to 24; 50 to 70.

A most beautiful tree, with dense green foliage, of general occurrence in the moist low scrubs bordering the coast. The wood is hard, close-grained, and of a blackish color. It is useful for the cabinet-maker.

127.—Clerodendron tomentosum, R. B. 6 to 9; 20 to 25.

A small tree; wood soft, and as yet of no recognised value.

TILEACEÆ.

128.—Elæocarpus obovatus, G. Don. 12 to 20; 30 to 40.

A tree common in the scrubs on the banks of the Brisbane River; wood fine-grained, not yet used.

129.—Elæocarpus grandis, F. M. *Callhum*. 24 to 36; 80 to 90.

This tree is frequent in the moist low scrubs along the coast, the trunk is erect, the bark smooth, the branches, with their thin, bright-green, glossy foliage, are thinly scattered over its lofty head; the wood is soft and easily worked, it is likely to be serviceable for boarding.

LEGUMINOSÆ.

134.—Acacia falcata, Willd. 6 to 12; 20 to 30.

A small tree; the wood hard, and much prized for making stockwhip handles.

135.—Acacia glaucescens, Willd. 12 to 18; 30 to 45.

A fine species, of frequent occurrence both in the scrubs and in the open forest grounds; wood close-grained and prettily marked.

136.—ACACIA CUNNINGHAMII, Hook.
9 to 12 ; 20 to 30.

A small-sized tree ; wood close-grained, and takes a good polish ; found growing on the banks of the Brisbane River.

137. Same as 135 in a younger stage.

138.—ACACIA FASCICULIFERA, F.M.
10 to 16 ; 30 to 40.

A small beautiful tree ; timber close-grained, tough, and light.

139.—ACACIA SALICINA, Lindl.
6 to 12 ; 30 to 40.

A handsome-sized tree, in scrubby land on the Darling Downs District ; timber close-grained and nicely marked.

140.—ACACIA IMPLEXA, Benth.
12 to 16 ; 30 to 40.

A small-sized glebous tree ; open forest ground ; wood hard and close-grained.

141.—ACACIA HARPOPHYLLA, F.M.
12 to 20 ; 40 to 70.

A tall erect tree of general occurrence in the rosewood scrubs, near Ipswich ; wood hard, heavy, close-grained, and of a dark pale color, giving a strong odor of violets.

142.—Same as 141 in a younger stage.

143.—ACACIA EXCELSA, Benth. *Brigalow.* 20 to 30 ; 50 to 80.

This species covers immense tracts of rich scrub land ; wood hard, close-grained, and of a dark color ; in use for building purposes, fencing, &c., &c.

144.—ACACIA NERIIFOLIA, A. Cunn.
6 to 12 ; 20 to 30.

Small but handsome tree ; wood close and prettily marked ; open forest ground on the Darling Downs.

145.—ACACIA DORATOXYLON, A. Cunn.
6 to 12 ; 25 to 35.

In scrubs and open forest ground on the Darling Downs ; wood hard, close-grained.

146.—ACACIA PENDULA, A. Cunn. *Weeping Myall.*
6 to 12 ; 20 to 35.

A small and gracefully weeping tree ; well known for its violet scented wood, which is hard, close-grained, and beautifully marked ; used by cabinet makers and turners ; in high repute for tobacco pipes ; of frequent occurrence in the Darling Downs.

147.—ACACIA STENOPHYLLA, A. Cunn. *Ironwood.* 15 to 24 ; 40 to 60.

This species is scantily scattered over the open forest ground on the Darling Downs ; timber is very hard, heavy, close-grained, beautifully marked, black, and will take a fine polish.

148.—Same as 145. From R. F. Walker, Gowrie Creek.

149.—ACACIA LEPTOSTACHYA, Benth.
4 to 10 ; 20 to 25.

Not unfrequent in the Darling Downs.

150.—ACACIA UNCIFERA, Benth.
3 to 5 ; 6 to 10.

Occurring on sandstone rocks, near Laidley.

151.—ACACIA DECURRENS, Willd. *Green Wattle.* 3 to 8 ; 30 to 40.

A beautiful tree ; frequent throughout the colony ; the bark is much prized for tanning ; wood strong, light, and tough.

152.—ACACIA AMBLYGONA, A. Cunn.
6 to 10 ; 20 to 25.

Open forest ground near the Brisbane and Albert Rivers.

153.—ACACIA STRIATA, Hill. 6 to 18 ; 40 to 50.

This very handsome, slender, erect tree is only known from McLean Scrub upon the Albert River ; the trunk is beautifully striated with green and white. The Duramen is of a light-yellow color, not unlike the yellow wood of the colonists, but harder.

154.—ACACIA DECURRENS, VAR. MOLLIS, Lindl. *Silver Wattle.* 6 to 10 ; 30 to 40.

This species is of very frequent occurrence through the Darling Downs district ; and bark much prized for tanning.

155.—ALBIZZIA THOZETIANA, F. M.
12 to 30 ; 40 to 60.

A tree of common occurrence in stony scrubs in the Kennedy District. Timber very hard, heavy, tough, and close-grained. May prove useful for gun stocks, &c., &c.

162.—ACACIA LINIFOLIA, Willd.
3 to 4 ; 10 to 15.

A tall, slender, graceful shrub, of common occurrence in the neighborhood of Brisbane ; wood close and light.

163.—ACACIA PENNINERVIS, Sieb.
2 to 4 ; 6 to 12.

Scattered through open stony ridges. Bark much prized for tanning.

219.—PITHECOLOBIUM PRUINOSUM, Benth.
5 to 12 ; 40 to 50.

In moist low scrubs on the coast. Wood soft ; not durable.

222.—HOVEA ACUTIFOLIA, A. Cunn.
2 to 4 ; 6 to 10.

A beautiful shrub, of frequent occurrence.

156.—CASTANOSPERMUM AUSTRALE, A. Cunn. *Moreton Bay Chesnut.* 24 to 36 ; 80 to 90.

A magnificent ornamental tree, with large pinnate, green glossy leaves ; of frequent occurrence on the banks of rivers, &c. The timber is dark and prettily grained, not unlike walnut ; occasionally used for cabinet work, for which purpose it seems to be well suited.

157.—BARKLEYA SYRINGIFOLIA, F. M.
12 to 18 ; 40 to 60.

A handsome and beautiful tree, with dense bright-green glossy foliage ; on fertile banks and flats of rivers, also on basaltic ridges.

158.—CASSIA BREWSTERI, F. M.
3 to 6 ; 30 to 50.

A small tree, of frequent occurrence in the Brigalow scrubs ; wood fine-grained.

159.—JACKSONIA SCOPARIA, R. B. *Dogwood.* 3 to 8 ; 10 to 15.

A tall shrub or small tree ; its local name of the offensive odor emitted by it when burning.

160.—GALACTIA TENUIFLORA, Willd.
3 to 9; 200 to 300.

An immense woody climber, outgrowing the tallest trees in the moist scrubs; the trunk is often found coiled on the ground like a huge serpent: the wood is dark-brown, soft, spongy, and pervaded with numerous capillary tubes; apparently of little durability.

170.—PELTOPHORUM FERRUIGINEUM, Benth.
24 to 30; 40 to 80.

A large and handsome tree, in the open forest ground on the banks of Mackay; the timber is much in request for cabinet work, &c., &c.

164.—ERYTHRINA VESPERTILIO, Benth. *Coral Tree.*
12 to 15; 30 to 40.

Rather frequent both on the coast and in the interior; a beautiful tree when in flower; wood soft, and is used by the aborigines for making their shields.

CORNACÆ.

170.*—MARLEA VITIENSIS, Benth. *Musk Tree.* 6 to 12; 20 to 30.

A small-sized tree, generally with a gouty trunk; bark dark-colored, rough and scaly; wood bright-yellow, with a fine undulating appearance, black at the centre; found in moist low scrubs.

JASMINCEÆ.

171.—OLEA PANICULATA, R. B. *Native Olive.* 18 to 24; 50 to 70.

A moderate-sized tree, of frequent occurrence in the scrubs both on the coast and also in the interior; timber close-grained, hard, and durable.

172.—NOTELŒA OVATA, R.B. *Dunga Vunga.* 6 to 12; 20 to 30.

A slender tree, found in scrubs; wood close-grained.

173.—NOTELŒA LONGIFOLIA, Vent.
12 to 18; 30 to 40.

A small tree; timber hard, close-grained.

174.—NOTELŒA MICROCARPA, R.B.
9 to 12; 30 to 45.

A tree of frequent occurrence on the borders of scrubs on the coast; wood hard and close-grained.

LAURINEÆ.

175.—ENDIANDEA PUBENS, Meissn.
18 to 24; 40 to 70.

A moderate-sized tree, of general occurrence in the scrubs on the banks of the Brisbane and Albert Rivers; timber not as yet used.

176.—TETRANTHERA FERUIGENEA, R. B. 14 to 20; 30 to 40.

Wood close-grained; not used.

178.—TETRANTHERA RETICULATA, Meissn.
15 to 24; 30 to 60.

A tree of frequent occurrence; the timber not used for any purpose.

177.—LITSŒA DEALBATA, Nees.
18 to 24; 40 to 60.

In favorable situations this tree attains a good size; timber close-grained.

179.—NESODAPHNE OBTUSIFOLIA, Benth.
18 to 30; 40 to 70.

A large and handsome tree, with a fine canopy of foliage, and lofty cylindrical bole; wood close, firm, and hard; evidently a serviceable timber, not plentiful.

180.—CRYPTOCARYA PATENTINERVIS, F. M.
12 to 20; 30 to 40.

A small-sized tree; timber of apparent value, but not used for any purposes.

EBENACEÆ.

181.—CARGILLIA AUSTRALIS, R. B.
6 to 12; 30 to 40.

A slender tree; timber very tough and firm, and likely to be useful for many purposes.

183.—MABA FASCICULATA, F. M.
18 to 24; 60 to 80.

A beautiful tree, of common occurrence in the scrubs bordering on river banks; wood tolerably close-grained.

D

EUPHORBIACEÆ.

184.—BALOGHIA LUCIDA, Endl. *Bloodwood.* 8 to 16; 30 to 40.

A small-sized tree, abundant in the coast scrubs; timber not used.

185.—MALLOTUS PHILLIPPINENSIS, J. Mull. 6 to 14; 30 to 45.

A small tree, generally found in rich scrubs. Wood close-grained and very tough.

186.—MALLOTUS CLAOXYLOIDES, J. Mull. 9 to 16; 15 to 30.

A slender handsome tree, occurring both in moist low scrubs, and also among rocks in dry places. Wood hard, white, and close-grained.

187.—MALLOTUS NESOPHILUS, J. Mull. 12 to 18; 35 to 45.

Of frequent occurrence in low moist scrubs along the coast. Wood of a uniform white color, soft, and easily worked.

188.—CROTON INSULARIS, Baill. *Cascarilla.* 8 to 12; 30 to 40.

A small-sized tree, bark grey and rough, with a red sap. Wood of a yellowish-white color; wood soft, and of no value; the bark contains an agreeable bitter.

189.—CŒLEBOGYNE ILICIFOLIA, J. Sm. 2 to 4; 6 to 14.

A pretty shrub, of frequent occurrence in the scrubs on the coast, as well as in the interior. Wood hard, and close-grained.

190.—CROTON VERREAUXII, Baill. 3 to 5; 15 to 20.

A tall shrub, found in low moist scrubs. Wood of a greenish color when cut, hard and fine-grained.

191.—PETALOSTIGMA QUADVOLOCULARE, F. M. *Crab Tree.* 12 to 18; 40 to 50.

This beautiful weeping tree is found in great abundance, growing on poor sandy soil in the open forests. The wood is hard, fine-grained, and promises to be useful to the cabinet-maker; the bark contains a very powerful bitter, and is said to have the same properties as the Peruvian bark.

192.—Excœcaria Agallocha, Linn. *River Poisonous Tree.* 6 to 18 ; 20 to 30.

Found bordering the estuaries of salt-water rivers and creeks ; produces by incision in the bark an acrid milky juice ; a single drop falling into the eyes will cause great pain, and, it is believed, will cause loss of sight. Wood light, white and soft.

193.—Bridelia exaltata, F. M. 12 to 18 ; 30 to 45.

A fine tree, not unfrequent in the coast moist low scrubs. Timber hard, close-grained.

194.—Bradleia Australis, R. B. 12 to 18; 13 to 50.

A tree of frequent occurrence in the low moist scrubs. Wood close-grained, of a reddish color.

MONIMEACÆ.

195.—Daphnandra micrantha, Benth. 18 to 30 ; 60 to 80.

A remarkable and very handsome moderate-sized tree, with bright-green glossy foliage, occasionally found in low moist scrubs. Timber quite yellow when fresh ; takes a fine polish, and is easily worked.

SAPOTACEÆ.

196.—Hormogyne continifolia, A. D. C. 6 to 9 ; 20 to 35.

A small straggling tree with slender branches, in shady scrubs. Wood close-grained.

217.—Chrysophyllum pruniferum, F. M. 12 to 20 ; 30 to 70.

A moderate-sized tree, sparingly distributed over the moist, low scrubs. Wood of a uniform pale yellow color ; close-grained.

APOCYNEÆ.

127*.—Alstonia constricta, F. M. *Fever Bark.* 6 to 20 ; 40 to 50.

This tree is of frequent occurrence in low moist scrubs, as well as in the dry Brigalow scrubs. Bark thick yellow, deeply fissurated, of intense bitterness. It is said that this bark possesses the same properties as quinine.

URTICEÆ.

197.—CELTIS INGENS, F. M.
6 to 12; 25 to 35.

A small tree of frequent occurrence in the coast scrubs. Wood white, soft, and pliable; used for hoops for casks.

198.—CELTIS PHILIPENSIS, Blanco.
4 to 12; 20 to 40.

This species abounds in moist scrubs. Timber not used.

199.—LAPORTEA PHOTINIFOLIA, Widd. *Nettle-tree.* 15 to 24; 30 to 50.

A beautiful tree; wood soft, spongy.

202.—FICUS ASPER, Frost. *Rough Fig.* 9 to 18; 30 to 45.

Timber of no apparent value.

206.—MORUS CALCAR GALLI, Cunn. *Cockspur Thorn.*

A rambling thorny climber; Duramen or Heartwood. Dark-yellow color, hard, and used in dyeing yellow and brown.

SAXIFRAGEÆ.

205.—CERATAPETALUM APETALUM, Don. *Coachwood.*
24 to 36; 70 to 90.

A beautiful tree, with long cylindrical stem; wood soft, light, tough, and close-grained, of agreeable fragrance; good for joiners and cabinet work; often in request for coach-building.

EBENACEÆ.

200.—
5 to 12; 20 to 30.

A small-sized tree; wood hard and tough.

RUTACEÆ.

201.—
6 to 12; 16 to 24.

Slender tree; wood firm and close-grained.

RUTACEÆ.
203.—
8 to 14; 30 to 50.
A tree of considerable beauty; wood soft and not much known.

CELASTRINEÆ.
207.—
4 to 6; 20 to 30.
A small tree; not common; the wood is hard.

RUBEACEÆ.
208.—
12 to 16; 30 to 40.
Wood hard, close-grained, and firm.

PITTOSPOREÆ.
209.—
2 to 4; 8 to 12.
A shrub of frequent occurrence in the Brigalow s crubs near Ipswich.

SAPOTÁCEÆ.
210.—
12 to 18; 40 to 60.
Handsome tree; upright growth, with milky sap, and bright glossy leaves; wood hard, close-grained, tough and firm.

LEGUMINOSÆ.
240.—
6 to 9; 20 to 30.
Pretty, small tree, sparsely distributed on the forest grounds near the Coomera River; wood hard, close-grained, and beautifully marked.

J. C. THOMPSON, Esq., Ruyanna.—
26 Specimens of Timber from the Burnett River.

Mr. WALKER, Townsvale, Logan River.—

    1 block of Cypress Pine.
    1 board of Red Cedar.

Mr. SIMS, Union Saw Mills, Maryborough.—

    1 block of Kawrie Pine.

Mr. R. F. WALKER, Gowrie Creek.—

    1 block of Sandal Wood.

The following articles exhibited, which have been made from Queensland wood :—

Mr. D. HUME, cooper, Brisbane.—

    2 model rum hogsheads.
    2 model tallow casks.
    2 model sugar vats.
        Manufactured from colonial woods.

Mr. WILLIAM PETTIGREW, Brisbane.—

    8 axe and pick handles.
        Manufactured from colonial timbers.

Mr. W. S. MACKIE, turner, Brisbane.—

EGG STAND—Foot of ditto, beech.
        Pillar of ditto, cypress pine.
        Spoon rack of ditto, ironwood.
        Salt cup of ditto, deep-yellow wood.

EGG CUPS—1. Tulip wood.
        2. Forest oak.
        3. Silky oak.
        4. Swamp oak.
        5. Sandal wood.
        6. Purple wood.
        7. Cedar.
        8. Rosewood.
        9. Deep-yellow wood.
      10. Black wattle.
      11. Moreton Bay chesnut.
      12. Light-yellow wood.

GUMS.

As is well known, a great proportion of the trees of Queensland, as well as the Australian Colonies, are "gum trees." To give a bare list of the Eucalyptus, acacias, and other plants yielding gums useful in medicine or the arts, would occupy considerable space. However, they are not likely to form staples of commerce until the population has considerably increased, and labor consequently become less costly.

BOTANIC GARDEN.—

GUM—*Xanthorrhœa arborea.*
Eucalyptus corymbera.
Eucalyptus siderophloia.
Eucalyptus maculata.

TANNING BARKS.—

1. Green Wattle—*Acacia decurrens.*
2. Silver Wattle—*Acacia decurrens, var. mollis.*
3. *Acacia Penninervis.*

———

COAL, from the Tivoli Coal Mine, near Ipswich, in two large blocks (boxes Nos. 45 and 46), exhibited by Messrs. Gulland and Co.

It is soft coal, 4½ feet in thickness; small band of stone runs through the coal 12 inches from bottom; sandstone roof. Wrought by an incline of one in five. Present depth from surface, 350 yards. Situated two miles from Ipswich.

COKE, from the Tivoli Mine, exhibited by Messrs. Gulland and Co. (boxes Nos. 48 and 49).

The coke is obtained from the small coal; the quantity of which is considerable from the soft nature of the coal. Specially constructed coke furnaces convert the small coal into coke on the spot. The number of furnaces is twenty-three, and the weekly production by them can be raised to 600 tons.

ALLORA COAL, Darling Downs, in two large blocks (boxes Nos. 47 and 50).

The seat of the seam of coal is 45 feet below the surface. The thickness of the seam two feet three inches. The distance from railway two and a-half miles. The distance from Brisbane 152 miles.

COAL from the Bingera Coal Mine, Bundaberg, Lower Burnett, exhibited by Mr. A. Walker, in one block (box No. 55).

For some years coal beds have been known to exist in the neighborhood of Bundaberg, a newly-formed township on the Burnett River, about ten miles from its confluence with the sea; but until very lately no effort has been made to turn them to profitable account. The small block of coal is taken from land recently granted to Mr. A. Walker, of Bingera Station. A small seam having been discovered in a gully forming part of a ravine about 60 feet below the surface proper; it was determined to drive into the bank in order to ascertain the dip of the seam, and also the quality of the coal. The result of this experiment showed three small seams of coal, which evidently will unite very soon into one. The thickness of the largest seam is 18 inches. The seams were found to be dipping to the south, and the further they were followed the better the coal was found to be. It is intended to further test the property by boring so soon as rods can be obtained.

The facilities which offer for the profitable working of the Coal Mine are not greater than those offered by Bundaberg in any part of the Australian Colonies. The river is available for the navigation of vessels drawing 12 feet at high tide, and can be navigated by punts and small crafts for 15 miles above Bundaberg. The A. S. N. Company's steamers visit the port regularly, and it is the natural outlet of the Mount Perry traffic.

COAL from Rosewood, West Moreton, in pieces (Box No. 43).

The depth of the seam from the surface is 39 feet; the thickness of the seam itself is 12 inches; the distance from Railway is 2 miles; the distance from Brisbane is 31 miles.

COAL from the Aberdare Coal Mine, in small blocks (Boxes Nos. 60 and 61).

The Mine is situated 5 miles from Ipswich and 4 miles from the navigable Bremer River; the distance from Railway, between Brisbane and Ipswich, now in construction, will be short; the Mine is 55 feet below surface, and the seam is 4 feet thick.

Coal from Flagstone Creek Coal Mine, Toowoomba, in two large blocks (Box No. 58, and exhibited by Mr. J. S. McIntyre).

Flagstone Creek runs west by south-west from Helidon Railway Station, taking its rise about eighteen miles from thence on the eastern slope of the Main Range, Helidon being distant from Ipswich 49 miles; the coal field is eight miles distant from the Railway Station at Helidon, over a comparatively level country, in the form of a half moon. The coal is cropping out on the east side of one of the spurs of the Main Range, and dipping westerly into the Main Range, at the rate of one in fourteen. The seam is at present eighteen inches thick, with nine inches of fireclay as a top strata; it has also four inches of composite band as pavement between the coal and under strata of free rock, rendering it in every way an excellent long-wall working field.

Cannel Coal from Blackfellow's Creek, near Gatton, in two specimens (box No. 56), exhibited by Mr. G. Harden, Brisbane.

This seam runs under the Main Range, and is stripped by the floods of the Blackfellow Creek, for the length of 400 yards, and shows a depth of from 7 to 10 feet along the creek. Distance from nearest Railway Station, 30 miles.

Fireclay from the Bingera Coal Mine, exhibited by Mr. A. Walker (box No. 54).

It has not come into use yet, but it cannot fail to draw attention for its usefulness in copper smelting, which is carried on at no great distance from it.

Impalpable Sand, consisting of exceedingly finely crushed quartz, mixed with infusoria from the neighborhood of Brisbane, exhibited by Mr. Petrie.

Pebbles in a bottle (box 56), exhibited by Mr. Franklin.

They consist of a mixture of cameos and agates, and form the greater portion of a conglomerate of siliceous matter, occurring in large blocks on Dykehead Station, Burnett District.

Pebbles in a small bottle (box 56), exhibited by Mr. Grossman, Spring Creek, Stanthorpe.

They are perfectly colorless topazes, and pass under the name of water-drops.

Ornamental Stone from Rawbelle (box 56), excelling in its pleasing mixture of carbonate of copper, flesh-red feldspar, and white quartz.

WHITE MARBLE, unpolished piece from Ravenswood, sent by Mr. Hackett.

It was taken from the very outcrop, which is two feet thick. The stone is very promising.

WHITE MARBLE ⎫
GREY   ,,   ⎬ From each sort one piece highly
RED   ,,   ⎬ polished, exhibited by Mr. Petrie.
VARIEGATED ,, ⎭

These four sorts of marble come from the Calliope River, 14 miles from Gladstone. There are many square miles of marble country between the Calliope and Boyne Rivers, in which very beautiful pieces of marble could be obtained of nearly every variety of color.

IRON ORE, in one large block (box No. 63), exhibited by J. S. McIntyre, Esquire, Toowoomba.

The ore is a kind of brown Hœmatite, and occurs on a spur of a range on the north side of Flagstone Creek, and is distant about two miles in a north-westerly direction from the outcrop of coal. The ore forwarded was obtained from a blow at an altitude above the coal of about forty fathoms, in a vertical position, as if upheaved from between the Silurian and old red-rock bands, and resembles very much the appearance of a copper reef. The seam is at present sixteen inches thick, and has unmistakable appearances of perma-nency. There is also a good bed of limestone about three miles nearer Helidon than the coal mines as at present opened. It is several feet thick, and suitable for smelting purposes.

IRON ORE, one piece (box No. 56), exhibited by Mr. A. Foote, Ipswich.

The ore is also of the sort classed as brown Hœmatite. It is found on the Bandamba Creek, a few miles from Ipswich, close to a coal field, two miles from a bed of limestone, and a short distance from a navigable river.

IRON ORE, two large pieces (boxes 44 and 63),   · exhibited by Mr. Russell, Pine Mountain, West Moreton.

It is common red Hœmatite. When the place was opened up for a few feet the ore improved very much, and seems to turn into fibrous Hœmatite. Its specific gravity is 4·78. The locality of the seam, which is several feet thick, is six miles from the navigable Bremer River. Coals are found in close proximity, and limestone is also not very distant.

MICACEOUS IRON ORE, in two pieces (box No. 56).

Occurs on the Cloncurry, in a depth of twenty feet.

CHROM-IRON ORE, several large blocks (box No. 53), exhibited by Mr. John Harris, Ipswich.

It occurs in close proximity of the Brisbane River, where it crops out in mighty boulders, for 200 yards, striking from east-north-east to west-south-west. This is undoubtedly one of the greatest deposits in the world of this ore. The formation of rock in which it occurs is the Serpentinic.

ORE OF MANGANESE, in pieces (box No. 52).

Occurs near Gladstone, is Psilomelane, and contains a small per-centage of Cobalt and Nickel.

TIN ORE—1 sample of large crystals in one bag ; 2 samples of surface dirt in two bags ; 1 sample of screened surface dirt in one bag ; 3 samples of lode tin in granite and quartz, exhibited by Mr. G. H. Davenport (box No. 51).

The samples come all from Red Rock, Ballandean Run, and speak for themselves.

STREAM TIN AND COUNTRY (box No. 56), from Spring Creek, near Stanthorpe.

BISMUTH, found in its metallic state on Chinaman's Flat, Cloncurry (box No. 56).

CARBONATE AND OXIDE OF BISMUTH, found in nearly all gold workings on the Cloncurry; chiefly in Chinaman's, Cameron's, and Sharkey's leads, Old Diggings (box No. 56).

SULPHURET OF ANTIMONY, exhibited by Mr. J. Honeyman.

It occurs in exceedingly large quantities on St. John's Creek, Burnett District, of a very good quality. It is intended to work the seam at once, and ship the ore in its raw state. Large masses of Cervantite occur along with the Sulphuret.

CINNABAR, exhibited by Messrs. MacTaggart and Party.

The Cinnabar comes from the prospector's claim, Kilkivan, Wide Bay District. They are, for surface specimens, very rich, and the mine promises well.

GALENA—one specimen, exhibited by Mr. Godfrey (box No. 56).

The rich specimen comes from Ravenswood, where it occurs very frequently.

GALENA—one specimen from Buchanan Creek, Western Creek, found during the erection of telegraph to Normanton.

GALENA with Silver—surface specimen from Staunton Harcourt, Burnett District, exhibited by Mr. W. H. Franklin.

VIRGIN COPPER, with crystals of Metallic Copper— several large pieces from Messrs. Sheaffe and Henry's claim on the Cloncurry.

RUBY COPPER, from Messrs. Sheaffe and Henry's claim on the Cloncurry.

Several large pieces, with splendid crystals of Cuprite.

COPPER ORE, 4 miles from the junction of the Duck Creek with the Cloncurry, consisting of Malachite in needle-formed crystals, and common green Carbonate of Copper.

The lode is 12 inches thick, on moderately high range.

COPPER ORE, exhibited by Mr. W. H. Franklin.

The specimens are entirely taken from the surface of the Central Alliance Mine, Rawbelle, Burnett District.

COPPER ORE from the Rawbelle Mine, Rawbelle, Burnett District. The ore comes from a depth of 20 feet.

COPPER ORE from Mount Alma, Gladstone.

COPPER ORE from Cressbrook Creek, West Moreton.

The specimens are taken from the surface till to a depth of 15 feet.
Two Companies are opening up the Copper deposits, at present, in the neighborhood of Cressbrook Creek, which is 40 miles from Ipswich, and coal is said to be found not very far from the mines.

COPPER ORE, in one large block, weighing one ton and a-half, exhibited by the directors of the Normanby Copper Mine, Mount Perry.

The unusually large size of the block of ore, shows how very rich the Copper Mines at Mount Perry are, especially the Normanby mine.

ANGORA MOHAIR.

One fleece, unwashed, from a pure Angora buck, bred by CHARLES CLARK, Esquire, East Talgai, Darling Downs (box 35).

One fleece, unwashed (box 35), from a third cross with common goat, bred by ditto.

One-half fleece from a pure Angora yearling buck, bred by the Honorable Captain SIMPSON, M.L.C., East Moreton.

One-half fleece from yearling female of third cross with common goat, bred by ditto.

> The cross in both the above grade fleeces was obtained by coupling a pure buck with a second cross female, obtained from the common goat. The sixth or eighth grade, by always using a pure buck, is for all practicable purposes equal to the pure.

WOOL.

Two fleeces, bred by LEONARD E. LESTER, Esquire, Manager North British Australian Company, Rosenthal, near Warwick (box 36), clothing wool, washed by hot soak and cold spout.

Four fleeces pure Australian merino, fine combing, bred by GEORGE CLARK, Esquire, East Talgai, Darling Downs (box 37), one in the grease, and three shewing the effect of different process of cleansing by steaming, hot and cold soak and spout.

Two fleeces in the grease, Australian merino clothing, bred by Messrs. HOGARTH AND BEATTIE, Balgownie, Darling Downs.

> The Commissioners regret that this—the staple product of the colony—is so meagerly represented. This was, however, owing to the fact that shearing had been finished, and the wool despatched from most of the stations, prior to their appointment. The three samples sent, however, fairly represent the characteristics of the acclimatised combing and clothing wools of the colony.

PRESERVED FRUITS.

(Box 39)—Samples of Marmalade from Queensland oranges, preserved in Queensland sugar, NEHEMIAH BARTLEY.

Samples of Candied Fruits—Rock-melon, Ginger, Pine-apple, and Candied Peels—preserved and exhibited by W. H. HAYES, Brisbane.

OILS AND ANIMAL PRODUCTS.

One bottle Unrefined Cotton-seed Oil, and

One bottle Refined ditto, made and exhibited by W. R. ALEXANDER, Redbank, Brisbane River.

One bottle Clarified Sheep-trotter Oil, MANING AND STAIGER, Redbank, Brisbane.

One bottle Albumen, the produce of one sheep, ditto ditto.

PRESERVED MEAT.

Samples of Preserved Meats. THE CENTRAL AUSTRALIAN MEAT PRESERVING COMPANY, Rockhampton.

Samples Extract of Meat (box 42) prepared and exhibited by ROBERTSON BROTHERS, Baffle Creek.

Prepared from best beef. Will keep good any length of time, even after having been opened and imperfectly covered.

All the meat-preserving companies had suspended operations for the season at the time of collection of exhibits.

COTTON SEED MEAL.

1 Bag, W. R. ALEXANDER, Esquire, Redbank.

An excellent food for pigs and milch cows, especially if mixed with bran and pollard.

LEATHERS.

Exhibited by T. B. Stephens, Esquire, of Ekibin Tannery, three miles from Brisbane.

1 side brown harness leather, 16lbs., value 1s. 6d. per lb.
1 side black   ,,   ,,   27 ,,   ,,   1s. 8d.   ,,
1 side sole   ,,   ,,   19 ,,   ,,   1s. 1d.   ,,
1 side kip, 8lbs., value 2s. per lb.
1 side black-grained kip, 7lbs., value 2s. 6d. per lb.
1 calfskin, waxed, 14½oz., value 4s. 6d. per lb.
1 black-grained kangaroo } 3¼ lbs., value 4s. 6d. per lb.
1 flat   ditto   ditto }
3 waxed wallaby skins, ½ lb. each, value 4s. 6d. per lb.
2 wallaby skins, dressed with fur on, value say 2s. 6d. each.

The above are Brisbane manufacturers' prices.

At the above tannery and currier's shop the bark used is from the acacia or wattle, growing wild in the colony. The tallow same as exported in large quantities, and the oil procured from whales in the Australian waters. About 400 hides (800 sides) of harness, sole and kip, are tanned per week near Brisbane, with a prospect of this quantity being doubled in less than two years. Wallaby skins are very plentiful ; there would be no difficulty in procuring a supply of 2,000 per week.